A TRIP to the GOLF COURSE

JESSICA SMITH

A Trip to the Golf Course
Copyright © 2024 by Jessica Smith

All rights reserved. No part of this publication may be reproduced, distributed, or transmitted in any form or by any means, including photocopying, recording, or other electronic or mechanical methods, without the prior written permission of the author, except in the case of brief quotations embodied in critical reviews and certain other non-commercial uses permitted by copyright law.

Tellwell Talent
www.tellwell.ca

ISBN
978-1-77941-456-4 (Hardcover)
978-1-77941-455-7 (Paperback)

Kaiser is a little over one,
And he loves hanging out with his parents.
Everything they do is so much fun!

They love going on walks outside
Or even just taking a car ride.

They love going to the park
And playing until dark.

They love running around
With their bare feet on the ground!

Kaiser just loves doing anything
He can do with his parents!

But when he first saw his dad hit that little white ball,
None of the other activities seemed to matter at all!

Kaiser wanted to hit the small white ball just like Dad!
So, he ran and grabbed a stick ...
And tried to give the ball a hit!

When his misses and misses turned into cries,
He looked up at his mom with tear-filled eyes ...
But his mom said, "Kaiser, give it another try!"

He stood behind his dad,
With stick in hand ...
Mimicking Dad's every move
Of toe wiggle, butt wiggle, bent knees, and focused eyes ...

When his dad started his backswing, so did Kaiser!
He had watched Dad all day ...
Hoping today was the day to finally hit that small white ball!

He heard a "Clink!" and looked up, abrupt …
The little white ball was going up, up, up!

He did it! He did it!
Kaiser hit the little white ball just like Dad!

Mom, so happy, gave Kaiser a kiss,
And Dad ran over and said,
"Woah! You cannot miss!"

Kaiser loves doing everything with Mom and Dad ...

But what he loves the most is being out on the golf course
And hitting the little white ball just like Dad, with force!

www.ingramcontent.com/pod-product-compliance
Lightning Source LLC
LaVergne TN
LVHW071733060526
838200LV00032B/491